UNDERSTANDING BLOCKCHAIN

Learn How Blockchain Technology is Powering Bitcoin, Cryptocurrencies, and the Future of the Internet

DANIEL FRUMKIN

Wise Fox Publishing

Copyright

Errors

Please Contact Us If You Find Any Errors

While every effort is taken to ensure the quality and accuracy of this book, spelling, grammar and other errors are often missed in the early versions of publication.

We appreciate you contacting us first if you noticed any errors in this book before taking any other action.

If you find any issues or errors with this book, please contact us and we'll correct these as soon as possible.

Readers that notify us of errors will be invited to receive advance reader copies of future books published.

Errors: errors@wisefoxpub.com

Reviews and Feedback

Reviews

If you enjoy this book, it would be greatly appreciated if you were able to take a few moments to share your opinion and post a review on Amazon after you finish reading it.

Even a few words and a rating can be a great help.

Comments and Suggestions

If you don't enjoy the book or have any feedback about the book, please let us know what you didn't enjoy or your suggestions for improvement by emailing feedback@wisefox-pub.com

We welcome all comments as they help improve the book based on your feedback.

CONTENTS

Bonus Resource Guide

Get the free Blockchain resource guide.

The guide includes resources to learn more about Blockchain, Bitcoin, Ethereum and ICOs.

A quick reference guide to understanding important aspects of blockchain and cryptocurrencies is also included.

**To get the bonus resource guide visit:
www.wisefoxbooks.com/learnblockchain**

What is the Blockchain?

For many people, trying to learn about cryptocurrencies and blockchain technology can illicit feelings of confusion, apprehension, or perhaps just simple boredom.

Developing a sophisticated understanding of how this nascent technology works takes a lot of time and effort. Fortunately, however, the basics can actually be understood easily when explained in simple terms, even for people who have little prior knowledge of computers or the tech industry.

WHY IS IT CALLED BLOCKCHAIN?

The easiest place to start with blockchain is probably just with the name itself. Why 'blockchain'? Well, as you likely deduced already, a blockchain is simply a collection of blocks that are linked together. What's important to understand is that each block contains information, and that information cannot be changed once it is validated and added to the blockchain. The only way that a blockchain changes is by adding new blocks to the end of it.

So a blockchain is a *digital ledger* of information that can be appended but not changed retroactively. A digital chalkboard that grows to accommodate more writing but is never erased.

On its own, that description probably doesn't seem particularly special or interesting. But when you add one word, suddenly digital ledgers become revolutionary. That word is *distributed*. And so, the phrase that most succinctly describes the essence of blockchain is *distributed digital ledger*.

Why does adding the word *distributed* make such a big difference? Because when you enable identical copies of the ledger to be stored simultaneously around the globe by anybody who wishes to do so, you achieve something called decentralization.

CENTRALIZED VS. DECENTRALIZED SYSTEMS

What do I mean by decentralization?

Let's start with what we're familiar with, centralized systems. These are traditional systems such as governments, banks, and corporations. They are institutions in which the power to make decisions is concentrated in a small percentage of the population which those decisions might affect. Or, in database terms, centralized systems are those in which the information in the system is stored and maintained in a single location.

Blockchain enables a different type of system in which decision-making power is not concentrated to a tiny fraction of the affected population. In a decentralized system, there isn't any individual or group that can decide who is allowed to participate or not. Instead of data centers full of servers that store information, the information is stored across 10s, 100s, or even 1000s of individual participants, called nodes.

One important result of decentralization is that it eliminates a problem that centralized systems have, which is single points of failure. If a corporation's primary data center is destroyed or otherwise compromised, the effects of that failure can be severe for the corporation and its consumer base. If the leaders of a government are incompetent or malicious, they can make decisions with negative repercussions for all citizens.

By distributing the information or power of the system, decentralized systems no longer have single points of failure. In this way, blockchain creates far more secure systems than were possible with previous technology.

How It Works

There's one more thing about blockchain that you should know before we move on. That is, how do blocks get added to the end of the chain? The key word here, at least in the case of decentralized blockchains, is *incentives*.

A decentralized network can't exist without multiple, separate nodes. The more nodes there are, the stronger the network. That being said, a majority of the nodes need to be honest in order to maintain the security of the network.

The original cryptocurrency, Bitcoin, uses *incentives* to encourage people to run nodes and to make sure that they do not have malicious intent.

The Bitcoin network encourages participation by giving rewards to whichever node successfully adds a verified block to the end of the blockchain. In other words, nodes process and distribute information through the network because they have a chance to profit by doing so. This is why nodes who add to the blockchain are called *miners* - they mine for digital currency rewards by doing computations similarly to how people mine for physical resources like fossil fuels and precious metals by digging into the earth.

But how do you make sure that the nodes process the information honestly? How do you prevent nodes from participating in the network so that they can alter the information in the blocks to benefit themselves? Simple, you make participating very costly. That way, anybody who wishes to attack the network by running multiple malicious nodes will have to pay a heavy price to even make the attempt. This mechanism for incentivizing only honest nodes to participate is called *Proof of Work (PoW)*.

By giving people reason to participate in the network, and do so honestly, Bitcoin and other cryptocurrencies have utilized the blockchain to create robust, decentralized financial systems that are already changing the world as we know it.

GAME THEORY

WHAT REALLY NEEDS TO BE EMPHASIZED IN THE BEGINNING of this book is that blockchains are a technological solution to a problem with human psychology. That problem is that when rational humans behave in their own best interest, as they most frequently do, it often has harmful consequences for others. Or to put it another way using the famous words of John Dalbert-Acton, "Power tends to corrupt, and absolute power corrupts absolutely."

Blockchains that are meaningfully decentralized cannot be controlled by any one individual or central authority. They are not just distributed ledgers of information, they are tools to incentivize honesty and transparency. A blockchain architect must strategically consider the possible actions participants in the network might take, and then design it in such a way that beneficial actions are encouraged and harmful actions are discouraged. This strategic decision-making process is commonly known as game theory.

To illustrate the point further, we'll go through an example analogy in which the blockchain is terrestrial rather than digital.

BLOCKCHAIN ANALOGY

Imagine you live in a small town in which, for whatever reason, everybody owes each other money. Now imagine that this is a time well before computers existed, when humans were doing the accounting and banking by hand rather than keyboard. Originally, all of the bankers kept track of everybody's IOUs in their own personal notebooks. Anytime somebody had to make a transaction, they and the other party involved in the transaction would have to go to multiple bankers independently to ensure that the IOUs were properly recorded and would be enforceable at a later date.

Obviously, this financial system is extremely inefficient for processing transactions and everybody in the town complains about it. Whenever an elder is asked why the system is designed that way, they say that's just the way it's always been. But as time goes on, the bankers begin charging more and more for each IOU they transcribe, until eventually some of the town members have had enough. They call a community meeting to discuss how they are going to change the town's financial system. Ultimately, they are left considering only two options.

One option is to designate a special record keeper who tracks every transaction and verifies that they are all valid. Having a single banker responsible for the IOU records would be a lot faster and easier for citizens. However, this record keeper would have to be the most trustworthy person in the entire town, as they would have control over everybody's finances. Not only that, but he or she would need to resist the temptation of enriching themselves by altering the IOU records in their favor.

The alternative option is that every transaction that occurs is engraved in a stone at the center of the town. A new stone would be added to the town center each day with all of that day's verified transactions. Anytime somebody wants to verify that a transaction is valid (i.e. that the paying party has enough funds to make the payment), they simply check the stones. Engraving the stone is a good job, so there are many town members who are constantly competing to do it. In fact, the competition is so fierce that if any engraver includes an invalid transaction, the others find it and take the offending engraver's wages for themselves that day.

These two options are very different from each other. While having a record keeper requires the ultimate trust in a person, the stones are practically trustless. Whereas somebody could go to the record keeper and request or perhaps offer a bribe in exchange for an alteration to a previous transaction, altering a transaction that's been engraved in the stone would be impossible. In that way, the stone helps eliminate one possibility for fraud.

For easier referencing and greater security, each stone that is added could have a unique and impossible-to-replicate identifier referencing the previous day's stone, which would have a unique identifier referencing the day before that, and so on. Once the day is over, the stone is permanently sealed, thereby maintaining the integrity of the records. Any attempt to forge and alter a stone would be easy to spot because of the unique identifiers.

But how do you ensure that the original engravings on the stone aren't fraudulent without putting too much trust in the hands of just one or a few town members? The answer is to have a requirement that more than 50% of the town agree that a transaction is valid before engraving it in the stone. Each person in the town can receive a copy of the stones so that the transaction history is easy to verify in the event an original stone is damaged or destroyed

The functionality of the publicly accessible stone record is essentially what the blockchain accomplishes digitally. The stone system outlined in this chapter may not seem as efficient as having a public record keeper in the town. However, in its digital form, the verification of transactions and linking of the blocks can be almost instantaneous.

Compared to financial systems of the past, blockchain technology can be implemented in a way that is more transparent, efficient, and secure. At the same time, it is far less corruptible because the rules of the system are enforced by open-source computer code instead of by self-interested humans. If power does indeed corrupt, as much of human history suggests, then shouldn't we design our systems to be resilient to corruption by preventing the concentration of power into the hands of a few people? Blockchain can do just that, and it's come in the nick of time.

What is Bitcoin?

"Bitcoin gives us, for the first time, a way for one Internet user to transfer a unique piece of digital property to another Internet user, such that the transfer is guaranteed to be safe and secure, everyone knows that the transfer has taken place, and nobody can challenge the legitimacy of the transfer.

The consequences of this breakthrough are hard to overstate."

-Marc Andreesen, Venture Capitalist and inventor of the first web browser.

Bitcoin is the first ever implementation of blockchain technology. It's a cryptocurrency, or digital asset made secure by cryptography, which uses a blockchain as part of its solution for being decentralized.

People commonly mistake the term 'blockchain' and the name 'Bitcoin' for each other. It can, understandably, take quite a while to get used to all these new buzz words that you're going to hear now that you're learning about blockchains. *Decentralization, incentivization, cryptocurrency, blockchain, digital asset...* and that's just the start.

You'll be familiar with all of the terminology soon enough, but for now let's just clarify that common mix-up between the two 'B' words.

THE DIFFERENCE BETWEEN BITCOIN AND BLOCKCHAIN

Bitcoin and blockchain are similar, but not fully synonymous terms. Let's start with some quick definitions for both, and then breakdown the differences from there. Bitcoin is a cryptocurrency which is built on top of blockchain technology. A blockchain is a digital ledger of information that can be easily distributed across a network.

In the first chapter, we talked about how incentives are used to enable Bitcoin's decentralization. The blockchain is what enables Bitcoin to be globally accessible, which is part of decentralization. But it is the incentives for maintaining and adding to the blockchain that prevent it from being controlled by anybody. Take away the incentives, and Bitcoin is no longer secure. It's value as a currency would plummet to zero, even if the information stored within the blockchain is still publicly accessible to people around the world.

A blockchain without incentives is simply a distributable digital ledger with a lesser degree of security and/or decentralization. For example, a large company could use a blockchain as a database to manage their supply chain. This blockchain might improve the company's security and efficiency. However, the company isn't trying to be decentralized, so they would control all of the nodes in their network. As a result, the company wouldn't need to use incentives like Bitcoin, and their network wouldn't resemble Bitcoin's all that closely.

Obviously, incentives are a very important part of the

equation for decentralized blockchains. We'll be discussing them in much greater depth in Chapter 4, which is around the time people typically start to appreciate the brilliance of Bitcoin. Before we get to that though, let's address another common misunderstanding people have when they first learn about Bitcoin.

WHAT MAKES BITCOIN VALUABLE?

Bitcoin isn't a tangible asset. It's not backed by gold, the US Dollar, or any other physical thing. It exits purely in its digital form. So how is it worth anything?

The best way to answer that question is to analyze what Bitcoin has in common with other currencies, and then what makes it different.

First, like other currencies, Bitcoin is transferable. If Alice owns Bitcoin and wants to send it to Bob, she can do that. In fact, such a transaction isn't entirely different from a simple bank transfer from one account to another. The key difference is that there isn't a middleman for the Bitcoin transaction. This type of transaction is called peer-to-peer (P2P).

Bitcoin is also scarce - one can't simply create more of it limitlessly. Its scarcity is actually much more similar to that of gold or diamonds than fiat currencies like the USD, EUR, RMB, etc. That's because the ultimate supply of Bitcoin is capped by its source code (at 21 million coins), whereas fiat currencies can be printed and inflated endlessly if the government that controls them is reckless.

Next is divisibility. Transactions in Bitcoin do not have to occur with whole bitcoins. Instead, bitcoins can be divided into subunits, called satoshis, which are like cents for dollars. In Bitcoin, 1 satoshi = 0.00000001 ₿. In other words, a single bitcoin can be divided into 100,000,000 pieces. Supposing that a single bitcoin were to some day be worth hundreds of thousands or even millions of dollars, a simple edit to the code could increase its divisibility further in order to keep it usable for small transactions.

Then there is durability. A currency isn't valuable if it can't stand the tests of weather and time. If you've ever left some cash in your pocket and put your clothes through the washing machine, then you know exactly why durability is an important property for currency. For Bitcoin, as long as the network survives, all of the currency on it will survive.

Finally, there's fungibility. 1 kilogram of pure gold is the same value as any other kilogram of pure gold. 1 dollar is the same value as every other dollar. Likewise, 1 bitcoin is worth the same as every other bitcoin at any given moment. For an example on non-fungible assets, consider diamonds. Each stone has unique characteristics that make it impossible to assign a value based on any single metric. You can't simply determine a diamond's value by the number of carats it has, or by its color, cut, or clarity. You must consider all of those characteristics together and have some expertise in doing so in order to properly value a diamond. As a result, diamonds would make for a terrible currency regardless of how nice they might look on a watch or necklace.

Those 5 properties are fundamental for an asset to serve as a currency, and Bitcoin checks all five boxes. That being the case, Bitcoin's value will be a simple matter of supply and demand. If more people want bitcoins than there are bitcoins available, the value goes up. If the opposite is true, the value goes down.

The final question, then, is why would people want to own Bitcoin? All of our financial infrastructure was designed for fiat currencies, so why would people want to use something else without robust infrastructure?

This question actually has several good answers. First is that Bitcoin stacks up well to fiat currencies in the five properties discussed above. It is more scarce and durable, more easily divisible and globally transferable, and at least as exchangeable because of its fungibility. You could even argue that it's more exchangeable, as there is no way to counterfeit Bitcoin. But the best answer isn't any of those things. It's that Bitcoin is *trustless*.

Humans are flawed. We can be greedy, corrupt, dishonest, and just plain incompetent. Human institutions like central banks and governments that control the flow of money fall somewhere on a spectrum of trustworthiness. The Venezuelan government would obviously be on the bad side of that spectrum after they hyperinflated their currency and wreaked havoc on their economy, whereas the European Union might be on the trustworthy side of the spectrum.

But at the very end of the trustworthiness spectrum, you have trustlessness - the absence of a need to trust. Bitcoin is a network that's not controlled by anybody. Its code is open-source and you can run a node on the Bitcoin network if you so choose. Using Bitcoin does not require you to trust another human being or human controlled institution. That, ultimately, is what differentiates it from other currencies.

The History (and the Future) of Blockchains and Bitcoin

"Cryptology represents the future of privacy [and] by implication [it] also represents the future of money, and the future of banking and finance."
- Orlin Grabbe, Economist

E lectronic payments systems have existed for a relatively long time. Amazon was founded as an online marketplace in 1994, with systems like ECash and CyberCoin coming shortly afterwards in 1996. Surprisingly, the idea for blockchains was conceived even earlier. In a 1991 entry to the Journal of Cryptography, Stuart Haber and Scott Stornetta described their idea for the first mathematically sound and computationally practical way to time-stamp data.

And yet, it wasn't until the Bitcoin whitepaper was published in 2008 that the ideas of a digital currency and a blockchain were put together and introduced to the world.

SATOSHI NAKAMOTO

Bitcoin's origin story is rather interesting. More specifically, it's the story of Bitcoin's creator that makes it so unique.

You see, nobody knows who the creator of Bitcoin really is. The Bitcoin whitepaper, titled *Bitcoin: A Peer to Peer Electronic Cash System*, was authored by somebody named Satoshi Nakamoto. However, that name is just a pseudonym that the creator used to communicate with cryptographers and developers online.

When questioned through email and chat forums on the matter of his anonymity, Nakamoto said that he chose to be anonymous so that his invention would remain separate from its creator. And you'll probably agree that his choice is rather fitting considering that his invention was a decentralized network that no one person or entity can control.

Nakamoto began running the Bitcoin code in 2009 and was the first miner. In the genesis block, he left the message, "The Times, 3 January 2009, Chancellor on brink of second bailout for bank". This references an article about the government bailouts of banks during the Great Recession, a political statement by Nakamoto about the institutions that his creation is now disrupting.

With the Bitcoin network running smoothly and growing fast, Nakamoto stopped communicating online in 2011. He is believed to own some 1 million bitcoins, but hasn't moved or exchanged any of them as of this book's publication. Given Bitcoin's volatility, it's hard to say what his net worth will be when you read this. As of December, 2017, it is well over $10 billion.

We may never know the true identity of Satoshi Nakamoto. Based on the times of his online correspondences, many speculate that he must have been based in North America. Even this is disputable though, as the article he referenced in the genesis block is from a British paper, and his pseudonym is obviously Japanese. Whatever the case,

Nakamoto will surely go down as one of the most influential inventors in modern human history.

THE TECHNOLOGY

Bitcoin is to blockchain what email was to the internet - the first killer application. And so, as Bitcoin's price made its first significant climb in 2013-2014, innovators and investors began taking a much deeper interest in its underlying technology.

Blockchain became a major buzzword in the tech industry as people began working on projects to utilize blockchains for all sorts of non-financial applications. These included identity verification, property rights, medical records, supply chain management, and more.

Because of all this development, we now have two classes of blockchains. First, there are public blockchains like Bitcoin that are available for anybody to see and participate in. Then there are private blockchains that are not decentralized, such as a blockchain used by a company to manage their supply chain.

Many people would argue that private blockchains are almost an oxymoron. If a network built on blockchain isn't decentralized, is it really any better or more efficient than other types of databases? That question is still up for debate and likely depends on the specific application.

Less debatable, though, is the question of whether or not blockchains will have a significant impact on our future society. It seems that we are on the cusp of a technological revolution of similar scale to the internet. Blockchain and cryptocurrencies will eventually develop such that they are a part of almost everything we do online. And yet, we will hardly even notice them.

How often do you stop while browsing through social

media or reading an article online to think about how the internet makes it all possible? Rarely, if ever? Indeed, hardly anybody outside of the IT industry spends time thinking about the internet itself anymore. We are all consumed by the applications built on top of the internet instead.

That is the likely future of blockchain. As the technology is developed and implemented in the coming years and decades, we will begin to notice it less. Blockchains may impact our daily lives in significant ways, but we won't really talk about them.

Where might we see some of that impact? Look first at the middlemen service providers that charge high fees to be facilitators, or that sell your data to advertisers without you seeing a penny. Content hosting services like YouTube that take a hefty cut of the revenue generated by content creators. Social media networks like Facebook and Twitter that can censor any content that they don't like while making billions from targeted ads. Blockchain can provide better alternatives to these systems and many others.

Of course, as the internet began taking off in the late 90's, few people predicted the applications we have today. Maybe the same will be true for blockchain, and there are world-changing applications that nobody is even thinking about yet.

Whether cryptocurrencies will completely take over global finance is still unknown. But the question of whether blockchains will have a massive impact on our future society is clear. It will, and it's up to us as innovators and early adopters to make that impact the most positive it can be.

How Blockchain Technology Works

"We have elected to put our money and faith in a mathematical
framework that is free of
politics and human error."
Tyler Winklevoss,
Co-creator of Facebook, top investor in Bitcoin

Y ou don't need to be a computer scientist,
cryptographer, or mathematician to understand
how blockchains work. This chapter will explain
concepts from those fields which are the foundation of
blockchain technology, all without using complex equations
and confusing variables.

From cryptographic hash functions to Proof of Work
mining - learning about these concepts even on a surface level
will give you a depth of understanding about blockchain that
very few non-developers have. In the process, you might find
that you develop a strong appreciation for just how innovative and powerful this technology is.

First, let's start with a basic introduction to the concepts
we will be covering.

How Do Transactions Work?

When a cryptocurrency transaction takes place, it is recorded as an encrypted message that is sent to the entire cryptocurrency network in order to be verified. When confirmed, the transaction is made public on the blockchain.

Each transaction - though rather complex - can be boiled down to three main components:

- An input - a record of the address in a prior transaction from which the sender in the current transaction received the cryptocurrency that they are now sending. In other words, proof of ownership by the sender.
- An amount - the amount being sent in the transaction.
- An output - The address of the recipient.

A WALLET ADDRESS - ALSO CALLED A PUBLIC KEY - IS SIMPLY a random sequence of letters and numbers. This public key is shared every time you send or receive cryptocurrency. Transactions are also digitally signed by the participating parties, using their private keys. Each public key has an associated private key, and one can only gain access to the funds in a wallet when they have both keys.

Cryptography is used to validate transactions with private keys. It is necessary to use cryptography in order for the transactions to be made public without any chance of somebody being able to figure out anybody else's private keys. We'll discuss this in greater depth in the next section.

The actors who do the verifying on the network are appropriately called miners. The verification process for most present-day blockchains is very computation heavy, meaning that it is resource-intensive to mine. Therefore, you have to spend money in order to make money mining cryptocurrencies.

Individual miners who are able solve complex puzzles the fastest in a given time period will put all of the verified transactions together into a block which they propose to the rest of the network. As a reward for a proposed block being accepted, miners are paid in the cryptocurrency of the given network. If a block includes invalid transactions, it will be rejected and the miner that proposed it will not earn a reward.

Accepted blocks are linked to the block that preceded them, which links to the block before that, and so on all the way to the very first block in the blockchain. The way that the blocks are linked (which will be explained in the following sections) makes it impossible to change them once they have been linked into the blockchain.

That's the whole process in a nutshell. Now let's dig into the details of the technology that makes it all possible.

CRYPTOGRAPHY

The data that we send around on the internet is often private and very valuable to us, a fact which is especially true when it comes to financial data. Cryptography is used to store and transmit that data such that it is only seen by those for whom it is intended.

Blockchains such as Bitcoin's are made secure in part by something called cryptographic hash functions.

Here's how they work:

1. Input a string of data that can be **any size**
2. The hash function will produce an output with a **fixed-size**, called the hash.
3. This computation must be efficient. In other words, producing the output for a given input should be possible to do in a reasonably short time.

TO BE SECURE FOR USE IN BLOCKCHAIN TECHNOLOGY, cryptographic hash functions should have 3 properties:

1. Collision resistance - It should be infeasible to find two different inputs such that the output of the hash function is the same. Technically, cryptographic hash functions can 'collide' (i.e. have the same output.) However, you would have to compute the hash function roughly 2^{128} times for this to happen, which would take more than 1 octillion years.
2. Hiding - given only the output of a function, there is no feasible way to know the input.
3. Puzzle friendliness - finding a value that solves a cryptographic problem for every possible output should require searching a very large range of possible values, guaranteeing that a solution cannot be found immediately.

ALL OF THAT MAY NOT MAKE SENSE RIGHT NOW, AND that's okay. In the rest of this chapter we will add in the context of why this is important in a blockchain using less technical and wordy definitions, and then it will hopefully make more sense. That being said, you may still want to go over this part multiple times if you want to really understand how blockchain technology works beneath the surface.

Now before moving on to that context, there's one more cryptography term you should know. That is, hash pointers. This refers to a value that is used to reference another piece of known information along with its cryptographic hash within a data structure. If you recall our analogy from Chapter 1, the hash pointer would be the unique identifier on each stone that makes it easy to reference and impossible to forge.

Okay, now let's start gradually putting all of that information together.

MINING

Blockchain miners are the ones who process transactions on the blockchain and mint new coins. This is done by periodically adding new blocks to the blockchain. Blocks contain information about all of the processed transactions, along with one additional transaction in which the miner sends themselves the newly minted coins.

It is absolutely critical that miners can't change the information on previously mined blocks. Otherwise, what's to stop miners from altering a transaction from some time in the past to give themselves more money?

This is where the cryptography comes in. Each block in a blockchain has a unique identifier in its header - the aforementioned hash pointer. Because this hash pointer is based on the outputs of the cryptographic hash functions within the block, changing even one tiny piece of information from a block will set off a domino effect that changes the hash pointer in the block header.

As long as each block has a hash pointer in its header where an adversary cannot change it, it is easy to detect a change to any of the older blocks in a blockchain. Each hash pointer points to the previous block, and so changing the data within the very first block or any subsequent block will affect the most recent hash pointer.

Can you see why the 'collision resistant' property of hash functions is important? If it were feasible to use two different inputs to a cryptographic hash function to achieve the same output, it would theoretically be possible to change the information from an old block without affecting the hash pointers. Since blockchains use collision resistant hash functions, altering even one transaction from any point in the history of the blockchain would be immediately detectable.

Miners can then be trusted to process transactions without altering any previous blocks. Additionally, it is easy to know whether or not a pending transaction is valid by refer-encing the last block in which the sending address was involved. If the balance left in that wallet address is greater than the amount being sent in the current transaction, then it is valid.

Furthermore, it's important that neither miners nor the public can figure out somebody's private keys just by looking at the blockchain. Otherwise, it would be possible to steal the cryptocurrency in somebody else's wallet.

In this case, the relevant property of cryptographic hash functions is that they are 'hiding'. This property ensures that somebody who can see the output (hash) of the hash function can't use that output to determine the input, as the input includes the private keys of the participating parties. Now every transaction can be digitally signed to ensure its validity without diminishing the security of the participants in any way.

The remaining question is, what's to stop a miner from including invalid transactions in the blocks immediately as they are mining them?

PROOF OF WORK

Proof of work (PoW) is a solution to that potential problem, and one of the brilliant technological implementations of Satoshi Nakamoto on Bitcoin. The idea is simple: discourage blockchain miners from even attempting any spam or malicious activity by making it extremely expensive to mine.

The high cost of mining is a strong economic incentive for miners to always be honest. If they try to be dishonest by proposing a block with invalid transactions, the other miners will not accept their block. Critically, that means that they also won't receive the block reward that they would be given for proposing an accepted block.

For a trustless, decentralized system to exist, it must be designed with game theory in mind. It should be expected that everybody participating in the system will act in their own best interest. The cost of Proof of Work mining is what makes it in the best interest of each miner to "follow the rules", so to speak.

Now let's try to understand how a proof of work system is technologically possible.

A normal computer can process thousands of transactions per second, and do it inexpensively. PoW systems use cryptographic hash functions with the 'puzzle friendliness' property mentioned earlier to make it more time consuming to process transactions.

In order for a miner to propose a block to add to the end

of the blockchain, they must solve a cryptographic puzzle. The answer to this puzzle is a value called a nonce, and it's impossible to know the nonce until plugging it into the puzzle. The likelihood of any given value in the large range of possible values being the nonce is evenly distributed. In other words, every value is essentially just as likely to be the nonce as any other.

As a result, the only way to find the nonce is to just start plugging in values from the range of possibilities until one works. This requires a ton of computational power. The primary function of all of that excess computation in the system is security, as the vast, vast majority of the computations will not produce the solution to the puzzle that the miners are searching for.

When a miner does find a nonce, they have the opportunity to propose the next block in the blockchain. Once they propose a block, the other miners can check that all of the transactions in the block are valid.

Now the rest of the miners can validate the block that was proposed. If they come to a consensus that the block is valid, they will reference that block's hash pointer in the following block that gets proposed. If, instead, the block has invalid transactions, the other miners will not reference its hash pointer in future blocks. They will choose to reference a different block proposed by an honest miner.

The invalid block will become 'orphaned', meaning that it doesn't become a part of the original blockchain. The miner that proposed it will have spent money to solve the puzzle and propose the block but will not make any money since the block wasn't accepted. Anybody who continuously tries to propose blocks that contain invalid transactions will eventually go broke so long as the majority of the miners in the network are honest.

ALTERNATIVES TO PROOF OF WORK

The cost of mining in a proof of work system is not solely on the miners themselves. All of that extra computation that makes the system secure still uses electricity, and using electricity has an environmental impact.

As a mining power (also called hash power) of a system grows, it's electricity consumption does as well. There is no way around this in a PoW system, as the electricity cost is necessary to make the system secure. However, there are alternative methods to achieve security without the excess computation.

The most common of these alternatives is called Proof of Stake (PoS).

In Proof of Stake systems, mining power is attributed according to the proportion of coins held by a specific participant. For example, somebody who owns 2% of the total bitcoins in existence would have 2% of the total mining power if Bitcoin were a PoS system. They have a 2% 'stake' in the currency.

Like PoW, PoS systems are designed with game theory in mind, anticipating that participants will act in their own best interest.

The game theory here is simply that people who own a large amount of a currency will want to see its value go up. Improving the performance of their investment is their incentive to be honest and make decisions that they think will improve the network. If they do something that negatively affects the network, such as including invalid transactions in a block, they are sabotaging the trustworthiness of the network and thus harming their own investment.

PoS removes the need for difficult and computationally expensive cryptographic puzzles, reducing the environmental impact of running the network. This doesn't necessarily make it superior to PoW, and it should be noted that the environmental impact of PoW networks like Bitcoin is often exaggerated by its detractors. Still, it's well worthwhile to experiment with other options and try to achieve similar levels of security and trustlessness.

Another, less common alternative to proof of work is called Proof of Burn (PoB). In these systems, the resource cost of proof of work systems is replaced by a necessity for miners to show proof that they have *burned* some coins. Burning coins just entails sending them to an address from which they can't be spent or otherwise moved ever again. This makes it costly to be a miner without having that cost come from electricity.

Of course, Proof of Burn cannot be implemented on a system immediately, as there would be no coins to burn. Even if a portion of the coin's supply was pre-mined before the network was launched, the coin would need to be valuable enough to make the cost of burning coins significant. Those factors considered, PoB would be best suited to bootstrapping one cryptocurrency off of another.

Putting It into Perspective

Not everybody who participates in a system needs to understand how it works in order for it to function well. The internet is a perfect example of that, as the vast majority of people who use the internet consistently have very little to no understanding of the underlying technology.

Blockchains and cryptocurrencies aren't especially different. The vast majority of people who adopt and speculatively invest in them will not know how they work, nor is it necessary that they do.

However, part of the beauty of this nascent technology is in its trustlessness. Blockchains aren't built and regulated by thousands of pages of legislation that only lawyers can understand. They are built with computer code that will execute consistently regardless of politics and other human influences.

By developing an understanding of the fundamental concepts in this chapter, you get to more fully experience the trustlessness of blockchains, because you know how that trustlessness is achieved. You can see Satoshi Nakamoto's vision for how his invention could change the world, and there is some beauty in that.

Benefits of Using Blockchain Technology

"At its core, bitcoin is a smart currency, designed by very forward-thinking engineers. It eliminates the need for banks, gets rid of credit card fees, currency exchange fees, money transfer fees, and reduces the need for lawyers in transitions... all good things."
—Peter Diamandis, Founder and Chairman of the X Prize Foundation

W e've already talked about some of the benefits of blockchain technology in discussing what makes Bitcoin valuable. However, that was merely scratching the surface of what all this technology can do to improve human society.

In this chapter, we're going to dive deeper into those benefits, beginning with the primary benefit mentioned in Chapter 1 - decentralization. To refresh your memory, a decentralized system or network is simply one which isn't controlled by a single person or entity. This means that a decentralized computer network doesn't have a single point of failure, making it more secure, durable, and reliable.

But what other advantages does decentralization through blockchains offer?

CUTTING OUT THE MIDDLEMAN

One important advantage of using blockchains is disintermediation - cutting out the middleman.

Let's say you want to transfer money from your bank account to a friend's account, or even just use a credit card to buy a coffee. In the first case, you must put in the request with your bank, wait hours or more likely days for them to process it, and pay a fee which can be quite large depending on the circumstances. In the second case, the coffee shop must pay a fee to the credit card company in order to allow customers to use the card in their shop.

In both cases, physical money is not moving around. Instead, there are just databases interacting with each other, sending one another bits and bytes of information. The institutions in charge of those databases are all incurring some cost to keep them secure. They also incur a cost when they must communicate with another database managed by a different institution. These costs are then redistributed to customers and end users in the form of fees.

Blockchains don't require a middleman service. Sending cryptocurrency from one account to another is as simple as copying and pasting the recipient address, typing in the desired amount, and clicking send. The miners will then independently validate the transaction for a comparatively small fee relative to that charged by banks for wire transfers.

By cutting out middleman services and replacing them with code, blockchains have the potential to greatly reduce transaction costs. The intermediaries are no longer necessary to provide security and trustworthiness, and that means there is less overhead costs for exchanging assets.

On top of that, there are not limited hours of operation for this process. You can send cryptocurrency from one address to another on Christmas day and the processing time and fee will be the same as any other day. Blockchains run 24/7, 365 days a year, making them more efficient in many applications relative to our traditional human-run institutions like banks.

But the benefits don't stop at lower fees and better efficiency. In fact, that's just the beginning.

DISTRIBUTED DATA IS HIGHER QUALITY

Over the last couple of years, it's become common for people to say that blockchains - and not the cryptocurrencies that use them - are the truly revolutionary idea. One could easily argue that finance and cryptocurrencies are still the killer applications of blockchains, but they certainly aren't the only applications.

Another emerging use case for blockchain technology is in supply-chain management. In this case, the benefits of blockchain are less to do with security and more to do with simplicity.

Having multiple databases communicating with each often leads to clutter and complications. By consolidating all of a company's data onto a single distributed ledger, the data is always going to be complete, consistent, timely, accurate, and available to everyone who needs it.

You can think about this like the telephone game. (That's the game where a secret message is passed around a group one by one until it reaches the starting point, at which point it's said out loud to see if it's changed from the original message.) Every participant, or node in the network, hears the message and then is responsible for passing it along to the next participant.

If you've ever played the telephone game, it's likely that you've experienced an occasion in which the message was significantly changed by the time it made a complete round. Each participant has the possibility of mishearing the message, or changing it on purpose to be funny. This process of sharing information simply doesn't have much integrity.

Now, think of what a blockchain looks like in this analogy. Say you have the same big group of people, but instead of passing the message around one by one, you just say it loud and clear so that everybody hears it at once. If one or two people mishear, the group can correct them and the mistakes won't be spread to anybody else in the group. That's essentially what a blockchain does.

In a supply-chain, using a blockchain would allow you to have a single database for tracking information from multiple manufacturers, warehouses, transportation vehicles, and store locations. The workers at every independent location that has company inventory would have access to the same complete information, leading to fewer errors and delays.

Still, the benefits don't stop there. In fact, we saved the best for last.

Transparency and Immutability

Once a transaction is validated and added to a public blockchain, everybody can see it, and nobody can change it or delete it.

The high level of transparency helps discourage things like corruption, and empowers the users of the system. For an example of this, you need not look further than the message Satoshi Nakamoto left in the genesis block referencing bank bailouts. It's now known that many high-up officials at these banks were paid millions of dollars in bonuses while economies crumbled around them.

Centralized and non-transparent systems will always have more potential for exploitation. Give people power, and the odds are non-negligible that they will use that power for their own benefit – possibly to the detriment of others. Blockchains offer a means of running systems without giving anybody power over them, and the importance of that benefit is hard to overstate. (Which is why I'm repeating it throughout this book.)

Another result of this is that blockchains are immutable, which is also called censorship resistance. This is considered by many to be the most important benefit of blockchains on a global scale.

Since nobody controls who gets to participate in a blockchain-based network, people around the world are empowered to have more say over their own lives. For some, that might mean being able to get a cryptocurrency wallet to securely store money when they don't have access to a bank account. For others, it could mean being able to upload identity documentation such as a birth certificate so that it will never be lost. And for citizens of countries that don't protect free speech, it could mean being able to voice their opinion or tell their story publicly when they would otherwise be isolated.

In this way, blockchains are a technology which can help the least privileged members of society to gain access to some of the benefits and opportunities that the more privileged take for granted.

TRUSTLESSNESS

We've already talked a bit about trustlessness in previous chapters, but it's worth repeating here. Blockchain technology enables peer-to-peer transactions where neither party has to trust the other or an intermediary.

When you receive Bitcoin to your wallet, you don't have to worry about the sender cancelling the transaction retroactively. You don't have to worry about millions of bitcoins being randomly mined one day and decreasing the value of the Bitcoin you've been holding. And, if you closely protect your private keys, you don't have to worry about anybody stealing your bitcoins either.

Fiat currencies require trust in the respective central institutions that control them. They require trust in humans who have power to not abuse that power. And, when those central institutions fail and citizens suffer as a result, there is little that can be done to hold people accountable. Cryptocurrencies only require that you trust code. Ultimately, that's the most clear-cut advantage blockchains provide.

Disadvantages and Dangers of Using Blockchain Technology

"Bitcoin is a fraud" and "worse than tulip bulbs.."
–Jamie Dimon, Chairman and CEO of JPMorgan Chase

I f you've heard a lot about Bitcoin and haven't heard people calling it a bubble, well, you might be living in a bubble. But if you've made it this far into our blockchain book you probably know that Bitcoin isn't a fraud and that blockchain technology is here to stay.

That being said, blockchains aren't perfect. As with most things, there are necessary tradeoffs and compromises to make in order to achieve all of the benefits blockchains have to offer. In reality, there are still going to be many situations for which blockchains are not an ideal solution. Understanding both the positives and negatives will help you determine which situations are a good fit and which ones aren't.

Let's get started with some of the challenges blockchain technology will face in the coming years.

BLOCKCHAINS ARE NEW AND COMPLICATED

As with any nascent technology, there is going to be a learning curve for it to reach mass adoption. Blockchains evolve quickly and have a lot of extra obstacles to overcome, so even those who know the technology well must put in a lot of effort to keep up.

Another side effect of the newness is that there is still a lot of uncertainty surrounding the regulatory status of blockchain based cryptocurrencies.

Currencies of the past have all been controlled and regulated by governments and centralized institutions. Financial institutions like Jamie Dimon's JPMorgan Chase aren't just going to go away in the blink of an eye. Nor should we except them to be early adopters of blockchain technology, as it is a direct threat to their business model.

While it's true that nobody can control a decentralized network, government regulations can still massively hinder the progress of cryptocurrencies if they are written and implemented poorly.

On the other hand, a complete lack of regulation doesn't seem like the best answer either. There are now thousands of cryptocurrencies in existence, and many of them are useless or outright scams. When large numbers of people lose large sums of money, there are going to be consequences.

Cryptocurrency enthusiasts can only hope that those who eventually regulate the technology understand it and its benefits well. Unfortunately, it's simply much easier to dismiss cryptocurrencies as a bubble than it is to try and understand them.

Speculation and Volatility

Yet another disadvantage currently faced by blockchains is the price volatility of various crypto assets.

While fiat currencies have values that are generally linked to their respective economies, cryptocurrencies and their respective digital economies are still in their infant stages.

The lack of real utility for crypto assets combined with massive speculation into their potential future values makes them unstable. That instability then makes them harder to use. For example, a merchant selling a $200 product would have to change the Bitcoin price of that product on a consistent basis to keep the same USD value. In 2017 alone, the BTC price for that single product would have ranged from 0.01 - 0.25 BTC.

It will take a lot of time and digital infrastructure development to get past the volatility and establish cryptocurrencies that are stable enough to actually use in everyday life.

For as cool and innovative as blockchains are, there is just no getting around the fact that their newness, complexity, and volatility are going to be disadvantages throughout the process of achieving mainstream adoption.

CENTRALIZATION ISN'T A PROBLEM FOR MOST PEOPLE

Supposing that everything discussed above weren't issues, would blockchain technology and cryptocurrencies quickly reach mass adoption?

Probably not. The reality is that most people in modern, developed countries simply don't care about or want the benefits that blockchains provide. Transparency, immutability, and transactions without intermediaries are all good things in some circumstances, but in most ordinary circumstances they are inconsequential or even negative.

Often overlooked when discussing the benefits of decentralization are the benefits of centralization that are lost. Most people feel better about storing their money in a bank where they can go talk to a teller face-to-face or call a customer service representative if they have any problems. And that's completely understandable.

There have been countless cases in the past where people

lost their private keys and access to millions of dollars' worth of cryptocurrencies. How many of those people wish that they could just talk to a representative at the bank and regain access to their funds?

On top of that, there are countless more cases where people were hacked and lost access to their cryptocurrency wallets. That money is almost certainly gone forever. Compare that to having a lost or stolen credit card, and suddenly centralization and bureaucracy don't look so bad. Banks typically block suspicious activity such as unplanned international charges until they can get confirmation that it isn't fraudulent. When fraud and other mistakes do occur, transactions can be reversed and your funds recovered.

If blockchain technology is to reach mainstream adoption anytime soon, there will probably be some layer of centralized control built on top of it. Right now, that can be seen in the centralized exchanges - Coinbase, Poloniex, Kraken, Bittrex, Bitfinex, etc. - where people are buying cryptocurrencies. These are all government-regulated businesses that serve as middlemen connecting users to the blockchain. It's a far cry from the types of use cases that blockchains are meant for and hyped up to be capable of, but it meets the needs of speculative investors for the time being.

The advantages of blockchain technology are certainly significant and useful, they just don't appeal to everyone or even to most people. Therefore, it seems probable that the technology's full potential won't be realized through mainstream adoption for a long time yet.

Ultimately, we can't have our cake and eat it too. If we want our systems to be free of corruption and censorship, we have to make sacrifices. With blockchains, one such sacrifice is losing the insurance that our traditional institutions provide. That being said, if there is economic opportunity to develop decentralized insurance applications for cryptocurrency users, rest assured that they will exist in good time.

BLOCKCHAINS ARE SLOW AND WASTEFUL

We've talked a bit about the various ways blockchains can improve efficiency. However, the truth is that blockchains by their very nature are always going to be slower than centralized databases. This is because they have to do all the same things as those traditional databases, while also achieving independent consensus from the majority of nodes.

For Bitcoin, PoW requires that the majority of computation each node is doing ends up being redundant. In a centralized system, all of that computation could go towards processing new transactions. But in a decentralized PoW system, the processing speed is much slower because it's necessary to waste computation.

An additional disadvantage of that slowness is that processing a single transaction consumes significantly more power in a decentralized system. Instead of having a couple nodes processing transactions like you would for Visa or PayPal, you have thousands of nodes all validating the same transactions. This is necessary in order for the system to be trustless, but it can send the total electricity consumption of a decentralized network through the roof.

On top of its costliness, the slow processing speed of blockchains has another downside. That is, once blockchains are being used by enough people, there will be more transactions per second than can be processed directly on the blockchains. This leads to longer wait times and higher fees for users.

It's a real challenge to maintain all of the benefits of blockchains while also increasing their speed. In fact, that scalability problem is the most pressing issue that blockchain developers face today. Brilliant solutions are being developed and implemented now, but there is still a ton of work to be done to scale these networks up to where they need to be to serve the masses.

Whether that sacrifice of the benefits of centralization is worth making will depend on the individual. The fact that we have the ability to make such a choice is progress in its own right, and that's all thanks to the innovation of blockchain technology.

Ethereum and Blockchain 2.0

"Ethereum has taken what was a four-function calculator of a programming language in Bitcoin and turned it into a full-fledged computer."
-Fred Ehrsam, co-founder of the cryptocurrency exchange Coinbase

E thereum is a platform that enables the development of decentralized applications (Dapps) that run on the blockchain by using smart contracts.

Let's unpack that statement really quick.

First, what are decentralized applications? Dapps are a variation of the common apps we use on our smart phones every day such as Twitter, Uber, or Gmail. What makes them different is that they operate without a middleman.

Smart contracts, meanwhile, are a variation of regular contracts, with the difference being that they are written in computer code instead of ink on paper. Because they are code, smart contracts can self-execute the terms of the contractual agreement on a decentralized blockchain network.

Much more on both of those concepts later on in this chapter. To get started, let's take a deeper look at Ethereum.

THE HISTORY OF ETHEREUM

The idea for Ethereum was first conceived in 2012 by a brilliant young computer scientist named Vitalik Buterin. Just 19 years old at the time, Buterin was keenly interested in information theory, sociology, politics, and economics. That, combined with his skill in programming and cryptography, enabled him to create his vision for a blockchain 2.0.

Buterin published the Ethereum whitepaper in 2013. In that document, he outlined how the Ethereum platform would work on a fundamental level. He also explained some of the potential applications he envisioned being possible with Ethereum. As it turns out, though, the reality a half-decade later has drastically exceeded Buterin's expectations.

In 2014, Ethereum conducted a public crowdfunding campaign to kickstart the project's development and growth. That campaign successfully raised $18 million in just 42 days. This was all done through a new form of investment made possible by cryptocurrencies, called initial coin offerings (ICOs). Investors in the Ethereum ICO funded the project by purchasing Ether, the native transactional currency of the Ethereum platform.

With help from other core developers, Dr. Gavin Wood and Jeffrey Wilcke, Ethereum launched on June 30th of 2015. By then, the community of Ethereum developers was growing rapidly, as was general awareness about the project.

The Difference Between Bitcoin and Ethereum

Between the time that Bitcoin went live in 2009 and Ethereum in 2015, many other cryptocurrencies were created. The majority of them tried to make some improvements on the Bitcoin protocol, whether that be enhancing privacy, increasing transaction throughput, or any number of different aspects. To the contrary, Ethereum doesn't improve on the Bitcoin protocol so much as it builds a new layer of functionality on top of it.

You see, Ethereum maintains all of the same advantages as Bitcoin. The Ethereum network is more secure, stable, and resilient than traditional centralized networks because it is decentralized. Data stored on the Ethereum blockchain is higher quality than that of a centralized database, with superior transparency as well as immutability. And of course, Ether transactions are trustless and do not require a middleman.

These advantages were discussed more thoroughly in the earlier chapter on *Benefits of Using Blockchain Technology*. However, those are only the benefits of blockchain 1.0. Ethereum is blockchain 2.0.

The major difference between Ethereum and all of those cryptocurrencies before it is that Ethereum is Turing complete. Turing completeness is a term named after English mathematician and computer scientist Alan Turing. We could dive much deeper into an explanation of what Turing completeness entails, but it's not critical for the purposes of this book. What's important to know is simply that Ethereum has its own an all-purpose computer programming language, called Solidity.

And so, where Bitcoin is like a calculator that performs a few specific functions, Ethereum is like a computer that can be used to run seemingly endless different applications.

You should also note that the cryptocurrency Ether is used to buy computing power on the Ethereum network. Total available computing power is limited, and so increasing demand for that computing power will generally lead to increasing demand for Ether.

THE ETHEREUM PLATFORM

Imagine if anytime an app developer wanted to build an app, they had to start by building an operating system for that app. Twitter would have twtrOS, Facebook fbOS, and so on. Most of the apps that we have today would be far less successful or simply wouldn't exist if this were the case.

For one, the development process would be too time consuming and costly to be worth it for most app creators. Additionally, it would be significantly more difficult to learn about and download the apps that do exist if you didn't have a general operating system along with an app store that organizes them all together and promotes them.

Of course, app developers don't actually need to build operating systems. Instead they use either the Apple or Android programming language and operating system.

Prior to Ethereum, the blockchain space didn't have a robust 'operating system' that could be used to create apps. Somebody who came up with an idea for using blockchain technology had to start by creating their own blockchain, and that made the barrier of entry much steeper.

Ethereum changed all of that by providing a blockchain platform that functions similarly to how Apple and Android operating systems function for centralized apps. Ethereum is essentially the operating system and the app store of the decentralized ecosystem. Just like your phone, Ethereum can run thousands of applications on a single operating system. Each app is unique, but they are all built in the same programming language and on top of the same blockchain.

In its early stages, the Ethereum blockchain predominantly served as a means of transacting. And, on its own, Ether was just another cryptocurrency with slightly different characteristics than Bitcoin. But as time has passed, more and more advanced applications are being created. With that, Ether has become more than just another ordinary currency - it has become the most widely-used medium of exchange in the entire decentralized economy, powering hundreds of decentralized applications.

DECENTRALIZED APPLICATIONS (DAPPS)

Many of the apps that we commonly use today could be closely replicated in a decentralized way. There are plenty of existing apps that are providing users with a good enough ratio of pros to cons that decentralization simply isn't needed. For those that aren't up to par, though, decentralization can be disruptive.

For example, YouTube video publishers who are constantly having their videos demonetized or censored could embrace a decentralized platform that is free of censorship and that doesn't take a substantial cut of the revenue. Disgruntled Facebook users who are tired of scrolling through news feeds controlled by machine learning algorithms might embrace a platform that is transparent and gives users control over the content they see.

Those are some of the more obvious examples because we use those apps on a regular basis. But there are thousands more possibilities. And Ethereum has made it feasible to explore all of those possibilities more easily than was conceivable before.

Dapp creators can develop the code for their specific implementation of smart contracts using Solidity. They can create a new cryptocurrency, specifically an Ethereum token, that uses the same protocol as Ether while being distributed on its own blockchain. On top of that, they can use the initial distribution of tokens to raise funds for their project through a token sale, much like Ethereum did with its own ICO in 2014.

In just a few years, we've gone from having a handful of basic dapps to literally hundreds of them. Blockchain technology has transformed from a ledger for tracking transactions into a tool for decentralizing just about anything.

SMART CONTRACTS

The last feature of Ethereum that we're going to go into more detail on is smart contracts. Smart contracts and dapps are inseparable. Every single dapp that's been developed is ultimately just a collection of smart contracts that add some specific functionality to Ethereum's all-purpose blockchain.

As briefly mentioned at the beginning of this chapter, smart contracts are a variation of traditional contracts that are written in computer code. Consequentially, smart contracts are fully autonomous. They self-execute when there is consensus that the conditions of the contract have been met, without any lawyers or governing authority being involved.

Smart contracts are trustless in the same way that sending Bitcoin from one wallet address to another is trustless. Taking trustlessness that one step further enables all sorts of new uses for blockchain technology. For example, you can have simple contracts that automatically pay employees upon completion of their work. Or you can transfer the ownership of some asset from seller to buyer as soon as the buyer makes the agreed upon payment.

It is not necessary to create a new cryptocurrency for every smart contract or decentralized application. Unfortunately, the ease with which one can carry out a crowdfunding campaign as an ICO has incentivized the creation of thousands of new coins and tokens that serve little purpose other than enriching their creators. As time goes on, though, it's expected that the majority of these coins and tokens will become dormant and useless, while the value of the coins and tokens that provide unique utility to society will skyrocket.

Together, smart contracts and dapps are already changing the digital ecosystem in radical ways. Bitcoin started the transformation in 2009, but Ethereum has taken over as the biggest driving force powering it forward. The question we're left with now is just how far Ethereum and its many dapps can go.

Use of Blockchains in Industry

"Blockchains allow the people to operate the network, merit based.
The people govern, provide resources, get paid in coins.
They create electronic gold, currency, financial contracts, without
rulers.
Internet protocols to allocate bandwidth, computing, and storage.
Self-organizing markets for power, water, Internet, and autonomous
cars.
Social networks and digital matchmakers without tech monopolies.
Bulletproof electronic ballot boxes.
Wherever a ruler is exploiting a digital network, blockchains will
disrupt."
- Naval Ravikant, co-founder of AngelList and partner at
MetaStable Capital

A s nascent as it is, the future proliferation of blockchain technology is still far from guaranteed. In an earlier chapter, *Disadvantages and Dangers of Using Blockchain Technology,* we mentioned that there are many applications for which decentralization simply doesn't make sense. It's likely that attempts to use blockchain where it doesn't solve a significant problem will ultimately end in failure.

However, development in the blockchain space has really picked up in the past couple of years. If blockchain does fail to disrupt a given industry, it certainly won't be for lack of trying.

While reading this book, you've likely already imagined some of the ways that blockchain might disrupt the industries you are involved and interested in. This is a great exercise, in part because it tends to be more interesting for the typical person than, say, cryptographic hash functions.

In this chapter, we're going to present some of the more promising ideas and visions for blockchain use in industry. And we'll start in the most obvious place - finance.

* * *

How Blockchain Technology Can Transform the Finance Industry

In *Rethinking the Financial Crisis*, economist Thomas Philippon of New York University states,

"Total compensation of financial intermediaries (profits, wages, salary and bonuses) as a fraction of GDP is at an all-time high, around 9% of GDP."

As global GDP continues to rise, more and more of that growth is being consumed by the financial sector. Meanwhile, one can wonder what the financial sector has done in return for that consumption. Has it been increasing its production to greater benefit society? Most economists will agree - no, it has not.

What does that ultimately mean? Well, it means that the finance industry has become increasingly more inefficient. A significant problem that blockchain has a chance to solve.

One place where there is an immediate opportunity to

implement blockchain technology is in asset management. Within this arena, there are brokers, intermediaries, custodians, as well as clearing and settlement teams. Each of them maintains their own centralized database that has to align with all of the others. The infrastructure is outdated and error-prone.

Simply by replacing those centralized databases with a single blockchain, the entire process can be streamlined and simplified. Cost savings would be substantial, with the added bonus of greater processing efficiency and transparency. Banks all over the globe are beginning to dip their toes into the blockchain world to cut settlement costs, including big names such as Barclays and Union Bank of Switzerland (UBS). All signs are pointing towards blockchains being a big part of future banking infrastructure.

Another opportunity for blockchain to disrupt the finance industry is with insurance. Instead of a cumbersome procedure of manually processing claims, policies can be implemented through smart contracts. This would lead to greater customer satisfaction and more timely pay-outs, while also reducing fraudulent claims through enhanced transparency and traceability.

Finally, of course, there's the matter of facilitating payments. Bitcoin was built specifically for the purpose of removing costly intermediaries from transactions. Where an international wire transfer through your bank might cost $35 and take 3-5 business days, cryptocurrencies can do the same transaction for mere cents and in a matter of minutes. Or, at least, that was the goal. The problem of scaling blockchains up to handle millions of transactions per second is proving to be a massive challenge.

Should the technology evolve to overcome the scaling issue - which is well within the realm of possibility - cheap, fast, and borderless peer-to-peer payments can become the standard. In cutting out payment intermediaries, a large chunk of the finance industry's GDP consumption could be redistributed for far more productive uses. That's why the original purpose for blockchain technology remains one of its most promising applications.

BLOCKCHAIN IN OTHER INDUSTRIES

Looking beyond finance, there are still countless industries that blockchain is poised to disrupt. We won't be able to mention all or even most of them, but we will talk about some of the more exciting possibilities.

THE INTERNET OF THINGS (IoT)

Perhaps the most promising non-financial use case for blockchain is as a decentralized infrastructure for the Internet of Things (IoT). This would enable smart devices to communicate with each other autonomously, a major efficiency upgrade. Big names including Samsung and IBM are working with blockchains for this purpose, as are many others. There are also several cryptocurrencies designed specifically for the IoT, the most well-known of which is called IOTA.

ONLINE VOTING

It's feasible and perhaps even likely that blockchain could finally enable secure online voting and bring democracy into the 21st century. That starts with developing a trustworthy means of proving your identity online, something which platforms like Blockstack and uPort are already working on. From there, blockchain can be used for casting, tracking, and tallying votes. Miscounts and voter fraud would become a thing of the past, and the improved convenience could conceivably lead to higher voter turnouts as well.

ONLINE MESSAGING

Online messaging platforms and cryptocurrencies seem to be overlapping more and more. The popular encrypted messaging app, Telegram, is planning to raise over $1 billion through an ICO in 2018. If the sale is as successful as most expect, it would be the largest ICO in history. Japan and Taiwan's most popular messaging app, Line, has also announced that they will be expanding into cryptocurrency trading soon. It will be interesting to see how these companies fair in the decentralized economy given how successful they have been with centralized products. For a service where security and privacy are paramount to users, blockchain might be the tool that takes these platforms to another level.

DIGITAL ADVERTISING

Another online industry in need of a shakeup is digital advertising. This sector is currently dominated by middleman corporations including Google and Facebook. As more people begin to realize how little privacy they have online, alternative services that value user privacy will have an opportunity to gain traction.

One cryptocurrency project, Basic Attention Token (BAT), was created to take the middleman out of digital advertising. BAT is built into the Brave web browser, a platform that lets users control and earn tokens for the ads they see, own their own browsing data, and many other innovative features. On top of that, content publishers in the BAT economy would no longer be subject to censorship or revenue splitting. This provides competition for companies such as

YouTube that take a substantial cut of the revenue generated by publishers while also holding the power to demonetize content that is controversial.

CLOUD STORAGE AND CLOUD COMPUTING

Modern-day cloud storage services keep data on centralized servers. That leaves important and potentially sensitive information vulnerable to attacks that can have widespread systematic consequences. As a result, decentralized alternatives are starting to pop up in the cloud storage space. There are even a handful of projects that have already gained a lot of public attention - Filecoin, Storj, MaidSafe, Siacoin, and Cryptk. For customers who want the highest security possible, blockchain-based cloud storage will be the way to go in the future.

On top of decentralized cloud storage, blockchain can also enable decentralized cloud computing. One project aiming to make that a reality, Golem, allows people to rent out unused CPU capacity in exchange for tokens. In the future, anybody with internet access will be able to generate income by selling their computing power and storage that would otherwise go unused.

REAL ESTATE

Buying and selling property is inefficient - full of paperwork and red tape. If the process could be simplified and streamlined, it would reduce costs for both parties in the transaction. To that end, a startup named Ubiquity has begun offering a decentralized Software-as-a-service (SaaS) platform. Land titles, property deeds, and other documentation can all be tracked and transferred through blockchain applications.

As for long-term renters, the process of finding a place

and moving isn't any easier. In crowded locations, prospective tenants often waste weeks or months going through countless bidding wars and rejected applications. Paying rent online is still uncommon, and even the process of searching for places and vetting landlords is more difficult than it should be. With blockchain, all of that can change in the future. In fact, an Ethereum-based startup named Rentberry is currently developing a platform to solve all of those problems and more. Soon, the process of finding or renting out long-term housing will be as simple and easy as booking an Airbnb.

HEALTHCARE

Healthcare in the United States and many other countries around the world is a complete mess. Hospitals and insurance providers struggle to communicate and share data with one another effectively. Blockchain certainly can't fix the mess all on its own, but it can help. By allowing healthcare institutions to share access to their data without compromising its security or integrity, healthcare can become both more effective and more affordable.

Several blockchain startups are currently working to improve the healthcare system, including the Gem Health Network and Philips Blockchain Lab. Hopefully, the future of the healthcare industry has secure and universal data-sharing, storage, and verification.

FORECASTING

Finally, we'll wrap this section up with a fun use case - forecasting. Accurate predictions and insights into the future are extremely valuable to society. One Ethereum-based dapp, Augur, is using blockchain to build the world's first decentralized prediction market. It's essentially an online gambling platform that harnesses the 'wisdom of the crowd' to make predictions more accurately than any forecasting tool before it.

FINAL WORDS ON BLOCKCHAIN IN INDUSTRY

It's still too early to know which companies and which cryptocurrencies will be relevant in the decentralized future. But the possibilities are exciting to say the least.

Many people have made comparisons between the modern state of the blockchain industry and the early stages of the internet. Might blockchain bring about a new age of innovation similar to that brought about by mass adoption of the internet, and of computers before that? Time will tell, but we are already well on our way.

Tokenization and the Future of Blockchain

"Governments will lose the ability to conjure money out of thin air. Budgets will derive purely from taxation and borrowing. Inflation will disappear. Prices will no longer rise each year. Bread will be no more expensive to a son than a father.

Humans will again build upon an honest, market-based financial system, having escaped fiat currency debasement, the most egregious financial scam of all time." - Eric Voorhees, CEO of Shapeshift

As of October 2017, Wikipedia was the fifth most popular website in the world in terms of overall site traffic. Including pages in all languages, there are over 45 million articles on Wikipedia, which combined receive greater than 18 billion page views per month.

Yet, there has never been a single advertisement on Wikipedia. The site operates as part of a non-profit called the Wikimedia Foundation and is funded primarily by reader donations. What could be one of the most lucrative websites in the world is instead providing immeasurable value for next to nothing in return.

Wikipedia is the incredibly rare story of a company that

had the chance to capture value and chose not to. In the history of the internet, a different story has been far more common. It's been the story of immense value creation with no means of capturing it.

While Google, Facebook, Amazon, Alibaba, and other online applications have grown into the largest businesses in the world, the people who built the internet protocol layer - the infrastructure that makes all of those applications possible - have received an unbelievably tiny portion of the financial benefit.

Blockchain enables programmers to capture the value that they create at the protocol level. We've talked a lot about all of the industries that blockchain can disrupt, but ultimately, it's that ability to capture value that makes the future of blockchain so incredibly bright.

Capturing Value at the Protocol Layer

Chances are you've heard somebody say something along the lines of, "I'm more interested in blockchain than cryptocurrencies." Or perhaps even, "I don't like cryptocurrencies, but I like blockchain."

If you hear somebody say that, it's as sure a sign as any that they haven't fully grasped the big picture when it comes to blockchain and where all of this is heading.

The first decade of blockchain's existence has been primarily about building the protocol layer - the infrastructure for the decentralized, open-source web. And, as the value provided by that blockchain protocol layer has grown, so too has the value of the coins and tokens that are part of those protocols, such as Bitcoin and Ethereum.

Imagine if the people who developed open-source protocols had been able to maintain the full integrity of their work and kept it open-source while also getting compensated appropriately for it. You'd more likely know the name Tim Berners-Lee, who created the World Wide Web as we know it with HTTP (Hypertext Transfer Protocol that connects web servers). Likewise, Robert E. Kahn and Vinton Cerf would be household names as the enormously wealthy creators of TCP/IP (Transmission Control Protocol / Internet Protocol). And let's not forget Jon Postel, whose creation of the SMTP (Simple Mail Transfer Protocol) enabled modern day email services and created trillions of dollars of value.

Without their open-source contributions, none of the applications we have today would be possible. And yet, their reputations and personal wealth pale in comparison of those who built on top of their work, like Jeff Bezos and Mark Zuckerberg.

To say that blockchain is good but cryptocurrencies are bad is to misunderstand a major reason why blockchain is good in the first place. In the past, the incentive for people to build things the Wikipedia way instead of the Google or Facebook way was no more than ideals and unselfishness. But with blockchain, everybody from the most self-interested person in the world to the least has the incentive to build projects that are open-source, transparent, and decentralized. That's true because of cryptocurrencies.

FAT VS. THIN PROTOCOLS

While on the topic of capturing value at the protocol layer, an ongoing debate in the blockchain space is whether or not individual protocols will be fat or thin. In other words, will a few 'fat' protocols dominate the future of the space, or will decentralization and the structure of blockchain lead to a higher number of relatively 'thin' protocols?

In pure database terms, there's a couple of reasons to believe that a few fat protocols could emerge. Looking at the web today, application level databases are where all the value is kept. Google and Facebook are nothing without the massive store of user data that they keep closely guarded. For the decentralized web, the data stays mostly on the protocol-level databases - the blockchains. It follows that the fat applications of today's web will be thin on the decentralized web, while the thin protocols of today's web will be fat on the decentralized web.

Another reason to believe that blockchain protocols could be fat is that they have greater 'awareness' about the applications built on top of them.

For example, the thin email protocol mentioned earlier, SMTP, has little awareness of how it's being used. If somebody wants to use SMTP to transfer money, they require an additional application on top of the protocol that is aware of the information being transmitted. The message, 'Send $10 from Alice to Bob', can be sent by the protocol, but it takes the extra functionality of an application like PayPal to actually carry out the instructions within.

In comparison, blockchain protocols can both transmit the message and have the required awareness of its contents in order to carry out the instructions. Once again, a thin protocol and a fat application in today's web can be replaced by a fat protocol on the decentralized web.

There's one really good reason to believe that blockchain protocols won't grow enormously fat, however, which is that blockchains can be easily forked. A blockchain fork occurs whenever there is a change to the blockchain's protocol. A 'soft' fork is one which doesn't require the nodes in the network to make any changes in order to continue mining, whereas a 'hard' fork is one which does require nodes to change their software in order to continue mining. because of forks, even when the majority of the value is still being captured at the protocol layer, it can be divided amongst multiple thin protocols instead of a single fat protocol.

That ability for anybody to fork a blockchain makes the decentralized web more flexible than today's web, and it's an idea worth discussing further.

FLEXIBILITY AND COMPETITION

With the modern internet, companies can cross a critical threshold of adoption after which point they have minimal competition or even concern of future competition. As a result, those companies can take optimizing for profit to the extreme rather than providing the best product or user-experience possible.

Let's take Facebook as an example. In the early years of Facebook, it was an exciting platform that connected people and provided a positive user experience. As its user base grew, however, it became improbable and then nearly impossible to conceptualize any other social platforms being able to outcompete Facebook.

Once that was the case, Facebook no longer had incentive to put users first. Rather than optimizing news feeds for social connection with friends and family, the focus was gradually shifted towards optimizing for profit from advertisers.

Now suppose that Facebook was built on a blockchain. What would have happened when they began using artificial intelligence to filter news feeds in a way that made users unhappy and unconnected? Easy. Somebody would have forked the Facebook blockchain. The fork - let's call it Facebook Classic - would stay optimized for positive human connection while the original went after more advertising revenue.

It would have taken billions of dollars to create a worthy Facebook competitor from scratch in 2014. To the contrary, forking a blockchain would take mere thousands. On top of that, capturing the value of that fork would be simple and easy by using a token, incentivizing tons of developers to do it as soon as or even before the need arose.

The important result of building the web on top of blockchains is that developers are incentivized to compete, giving users greater choice.

In our specific example, it would a choice between Facebook or Facebook Classic, (and possibly others). As more users grow unhappy with Facebook's direction, the Facebook user base would shrink while Facebook Classic's would grow. The potential for worthy competition is always present, and the vast majority of people benefit as a result.

That is what the future of the blockchain-based web looks like. Greater flexibility, higher competition, and better incentives for building protocols and applications that are good for users.

INVESTING AND THE PACE OF DEVELOPMENT

The internet was created in 1983. In the early days, adoption of the internet was minimal and very few people envisioned it becoming anything close to what it is today. For that matter, the dotcom bubble didn't come to fruition until nearly two decades later, in 2000.

To the contrary, the cryptocurrency space has been growing at an unprecedented rate. The total cryptocurrency market cap increased from $17.7 billion to $612.9 billion in 2017, a factor of 34.6. It was one of the greatest bull runs an asset has ever made in history.

Of course, the near vertical price movement at the end of that run was unsustainable, and the market corrected strongly.

Like the majority of the stocks that crashed during the

dotcom bubble, the majority of cryptocurrencies that arose during this hype-filled run will eventually fade into obscurity. However, some select few will likely achieve mass adoption. There will be failures like Pets.com, but there will also be industry changing companies like Amazon.

For now, market caps are built mostly on speculation rather than intrinsic value. This has created a cycle in which speculation leads to increasing token prices, incentivizing further protocol and application development. That development then increases the intrinsic value of the various cryptocurrencies, leading to even more speculation on them.

Importantly, pretty much anybody with an internet connection and some money to spare is able to speculate on cryptocurrencies if they want to. The low barrier of entry for investment - along with the cycle of speculation fueling further value creation - makes it such that the market caps of various protocols always tend to grow faster than the intrinsic value of the applications built on top of them.

Nobody should be expecting a repeat of the 2017 bull run anytime soon. As long as companies can add blockchain to their name and see their stock prices surge for no good reason, the cryptocurrency space will be full of useless and scammy projects. But as time passes and things normalize, the market as a whole still has a ton of room to grow.

TOKENIZATION

As we bring this blockchain book nearer to its conclusion, there's one last piece off the puzzle that's worth talking about - tokenization.

In the future, practically everything scarce and valuable in the world has potential to be tokenized. Stocks, bonds, real estate, commodities, digital content, and whatever else you can think of that could benefited from increased transparency, security, efficiency, or liquidity.

Diamonds are a great example of the power of tokenization with blockchain. They have been a historically stable asset, yet they aren't tradeable for the average public because the diamond market lacks standardization, transparency, and liquidity. By tokenizing diamonds and creating a decentralized exchange to trade them - as a project called CEDEX is already doing - it will suddenly become easier for an amateur to invest in diamonds than it would for them to buy stock. Until stocks are also tokenized, that is.

Tokenization makes investing cheaper, faster, more secure, and more accessible for people around the globe. Markets of real-world tangible assets that are currently traded by outdated and inefficient means will be completely revolutionized by blockchain. We may have left it for the final chapter of the book, but the significance of tokenization is hard to overstate.

FINAL WORDS ON THE FUTURE OF BLOCKCHAIN

The movement towards decentralized systems is still very much new, but each day brings greater clarity as to the future of blockchain technology and how it will impact our society.

In the coming years, we expect governments to get serious about regulating cryptocurrencies. It's hard to say what effects that might have in the short term, and even in the long term if the regulations are overly restriction and regressive.

At the end of the day, though, blockchain is nothing if not resilient. A government might try to shut down thousands of nodes in one part of the world, but rest assured there will be thousands more popping up somewhere else to take their place if it's economically viable.

The momentum and rate of development in the blockchain space are pushing it forward and building the decentralized web. And with a passionate, incentivized group of developers and enthusiasts leading the way - the future of the blockchain industry has never been brighter.

Bonus Resource Guide

Get the free Blockchain resource guide.

The guide includes resources to learn more about Blockchain, Bitcoin, Ethereum and ICOs.

A quick reference guide to understanding important aspects of blockchain and cryptocurrencies is also included.

To get the bonus resource guide visit:
www.wisefoxbooks.com/learnblockchain

Reviews and Feeback

Reviews

If you enjoy this book, it would be greatly appreciated if you were able to take a few moments to share your opinion and post a review on after you finish reading it.

Even a few words and a rating can be a great help.

Feedback

If you don't enjoy the book or have any feedback, please let us know what you didn't enjoy by emailing feedback@wisefoxpub.com

We welcome all comments as they help improve the book based on your feedback.

Made in the USA
Middletown, DE
26 June 2019